# NOW YOU CAN READ....
# THE STORY OF RUTH

STORY RETOLD BY LEONARD MATTHEWS

ILLUSTRATION BY ANNA DZIERZEK

**Library of Congress Cataloging in Publication Data**

Matthews, Leonard.
    The story of Ruth.

    (Now you can read—Bible stories)
    1. Ruth (Biblical character)—Juvenile literature.
2. Bible.    O.T.—Biography—Juvenile literature.
3. Bible stories, Juvenile—O.T.    Ruth.    I. Title.
II. Series.
BS580.R8M4    1984        222'.350924    [B]        84-15073
ISBN 0-86625-303-3

GROLIER ENTERPRISES CORP.

# NOW YOU CAN READ....
# THE STORY OF RUTH

The story of Ruth is one of the most
gentle and beautiful in the Bible.

One day a man named Elimelech
arrived in Moab from Bethlehem.
Elimelech came with his wife,
Naomi, and their two sons.

A famine had broken out in Bethlehem. A famine means that there is not enough food for all the people. That is why Elimelech had gone to Moab where there was food. In Moab, Elimelech and his family settled down happily. Years later, Elimelech died.

Elimelech's sons, Mahlon and Chilion, were now old enough to be married.

They fell in love with and married two Moab girls. One was named Orpah, the other Ruth. All went well for about ten years. Then, Mahlon and Chilion died. What was poor Naomi to do now?

Many years before, the famine in Bethlehem had ended. Naomi knew this. She longed to return to her home town. Orpah and Ruth decided to go with her.

Naomi, Orpah and Ruth started out bravely. It was a long way to Bethlehem. They walked along for many miles.

They were very tired. They rested at the side of the road. Naomi was a kind woman. She felt sorry for Orpah and Ruth.

Naomi thought of the long weary miles that lay ahead of them.

Orpah and Ruth were her daughters-in- law. Apart from that there was no reason why *they* should go to Bethlehem. Bethlehem was Naomi's home town, not theirs.

"You better go back to your own people," Naomi said to Orpah and Ruth.

Orpah and Ruth cried when Naomi said this. They knew that once they parted, they would never meet again. They wanted to stay with Naomi. Naomi shook her head. "It is a long and tiring journey," she told them.

"The chances are we will never reach Bethlehem," Naomi said. Sadly, Orpah decided Naomi was right.

Orpah said goodbye to Naomi. She started for home. However, Ruth would not leave Naomi.

"It is much better for you to go with Orpah," said Naomi.
Ruth would not go.

"Do not ask me to leave you," she said. "Where you go, I will go. Where you live, I will live."

Ruth loved her mother-in-law. "Your people shall be my people," she smiled. "Your God shall be my God. Nothing shall ever part us." Naomi saw that Ruth's mind was made up.

"Very well, then. Let us go ahead together," Naomi said. The two brave women went on their way.

In spite of all the dangers, Naomi and Ruth arrived in Bethlehem safely. Here Naomi was welcomed by her old friends.

Somehow Naomi and Ruth had to earn money to live. Ruth learned that she could find work as a gleaner on a nearby farm.

It was the gleaner's job to gather up the long stalks of oats or barley or wheat that were left behind after cutting the fields.

It was a hard and back-breaking
job but Ruth had spent her life
working hard.
She set to work happily.

The farm belonged to a rich man named Boaz. He was related to Naomi. Ruth did not know this.

Ruth joined other gleaners in the field. She worked hard through the long hours.

Ruth was still working hard in the afternoon. Boaz, the rich farmer, came to see how his workers were doing. The first person he saw was Ruth.

Boaz fell in love with Ruth at first sight. He sat down with his workers for lunch. He asked Ruth to join him. He wanted to know who she was.

"Where do you come from?" he asked. Ruth told him.

After they had eaten, the workers
went back to the fields. Boaz spoke to
them.

"Drop plenty of good barley near
Ruth," he said. "Do not let her see
you dropping it on purpose."

The cutters obeyed their master. They saw that Boaz liked Ruth.

Time went by. Boaz asked Ruth if she would marry him. Happily Ruth agreed.

After a while Ruth and Boaz had a baby son. How happy Naomi was to hold him! This baby was named Obed. He was to become the grandfather of the great King David.

All these appear in the pages of the story. Can you find them?

Naomi

Elimelech

Orpah

Ruth

Worker

Boaz.

Now tell the story in your own words.